NORTH CAROLINA PATRIOTS

Their Lives, Contributions, and Burial Sites

JOE FARRELL • LAWRENCE KNORR • JOE FARLEY

Mechanicsburg, PA USA

Published by Sunbury Press, Inc.
Mechanicsburg, Pennsylvania

www.sunburypress.com

Copyright © 2025 by Joe Farrell, Joe Farley, and Lawrence Knorr.
Cover Copyright © 2025 by Sunbury Press, Inc.

Sunbury Press supports copyright. Copyright fuels creativity, encourages diverse voices, promotes free speech, and creates a vibrant culture. Thank you for buying an authorized edition of this book and for complying with copyright laws by not reproducing, scanning, or distributing any part of it in any form without permission. You are supporting writers and allowing Sunbury Press to continue to publish books for every reader. For information contact Sunbury Press, Inc., Subsidiary Rights Dept., PO Box 548, Boiling Springs, PA 17007 USA or legal@sunburypress.com.

For information about special discounts for bulk purchases, please contact Sunbury Press Orders Dept. at (855) 338-8359 or orders@sunburypress.com.

To request one of our authors for speaking engagements or book signings, please contact Sunbury Press Publicity Dept. at publicity@sunburypress.com.

FIRST SUNBURY PRESS EDITION: October 2025

Set in Adobe Garamond | Interior design by Crystal Devine | Cover by Lawrence Knorr | Edited by the authors.

Publisher's Cataloging-in-Publication Data
Names: Farrell, Joe, author | Farley, Joe, author | Knorr, Lawrence, author.
Title: North Carolina patriots : their lives, contributions, and burial sites / Joe Farrell Lawrence Knorr Joe Farley.
Description: First trade paperback edition. | Mechanicsburg, PA : Sunbury Press, 2025.
Summary: The individuals from North Carolina who played prominent roles in the founding of the USA are detailed.
Identifiers: ISBN 979-8-88819-388-4 (softcover).
Subjects: HISTORY / United States / Revolutionary Period (1775-1800) | BIOGRAPHY & AUTOBIOGRAPHY / Political.

Designed in the USA
0 1 1 2 3 5 8 13 21 34 55

For the Love of Books!

Contents

Introduction v

Richard Caswell Revolutionary Governor 1
William Blount Founder of Tennessee 7
Thomas Burke States' Rights Congressman 14
Cornelius Harnett Hero of Cape Fear 18
Joseph Hewes First Secretary of Naval Affairs 22
William Hooper A Tory in the Continental Congress 26
James Iredell An Original Supreme 31
John Penn The Penn with a Pen 35
Richard Dobbs Spaight The Dueling Signer 39
John Williams North Carolina Speaker of the House 44
Hugh Williamson "The Ben Franklin of North Carolina" 47

Sources 52
Index 56

Introduction

During the American Revolution, it was far more prestigious to focus on state and local assignments than on commitments to a nascent federal government. Afterall, for many decades before and after, residents thought of themselves as citizens of their colony or state and of England, rather than a shaky new confederation that did not have the power to tax. Up through the Civil War, loyalty to one's state often trumped loyalty to the nation. Governor Richard Caswell, of North Carolina, was such a person. He was twice the governor of North Carolina and was an important figure in the transition of North Carolina from a colony under the English Crown to an independent state affiliated with the newly formed United States of America. His impact helped cement the foundation of North Carolina as we know it today and was key to the formation of the nation as a whole. Thus, though Caswell's service in the Continental Congress ended soon after the signing of the Continental Association, we should not think of his role as diminished as he focused on issues closer to home. We also thank him for his military service, leading in the field.

William Hooper and Joseph Hewes joined Richard Caswell for the First Continental Congress in Philadelphia where they signed the Continental Association on behalf of their colony. Hooper and Hewes, however, did not stop there. They continued with the Continental Congress and were signatories of the Declaration of Independence. Both Hooper and Hewes were transplants, from Massachusetts and New Jersey, respectively.

Taking Richard Caswell's seat in the Continental Congress was John Penn, a transplant from Virginia who was a well-known lawyer and no relation to the Penns who founded Pennsylvania. He stuck with the Congress as it was exiled in York, Pennsylvania. There, he also signed the Articles of Confederation.

Thomas Burke and Cornelius Harnett joined John Penn in York, Pennsylvania, during the most difficult days of the Revolution. Burke fought at the Battle of Brandywine and was a strong proponent of the Articles of Confederation but did not sign them. He was later a governor of North Carolina. Cornelius Harnett stayed in York and signed the Articles but was captured by the British upon his return to his state and died due to exposure in prison.

Patriot John Williams, who was involved in the early formation of Kentucky, served in the military and as the speaker of the North Carolina Assembly. He signed the Articles of Confederation in Philadelphia, after the Congress had returned.

Richard Dobbs Spaight, William Blount, and Hugh Williamson signed the US Constitution for North Carolina. Spaight, like Alexander Hamilton, was later killed in a duel. Blount went on to help found Tennessee. Williamson, who was born in Pennsylvania and died in New York City, was a renowned scholar some called "The Ben Franklin of North Carolina."

Of course, finally, James Iredell served as one of the founding members of the US Supreme Court. His son, James Iredell Jr., also served as a governor of North Carolina.

Please enjoy the retelling of our founding through the brief biographies of these citizens of North Carolina. Always remember: "Poor is the nation that has no heroes, but poorer still is the nation that having heroes, fails to remember and honor them." (attributed to Marcus Tullius Cicero)

Lawrence Knorr, Ph.D.
October 2025

Richard Caswell
(1729–1789)

Revolutionary Governor

Buried at Caswell Memorial Cemetery,
Kinston, North Carolina.

Military • Continental Association

This founder served as the first and fifth governor of the state of North Carolina. During the American Revolution, he served as a senior officer in the militia in the Southern theater. As a delegate to the First Continental Congress, he signed the 1774 Continental Association. John Adams referred to him as a model man and a true patriot. His name was Richard Caswell.

Caswell was born on August 3rd, 1729, in Harford County (present-day Baltimore), Maryland, at the seaport of Joppa. His father, Richard Caswell Sr., had migrated from London to Maryland in 1712. A descendant of English gentry, he found success as a planter and merchant. He also served as a county court justice, legislator, and militia captain. He and his wife, Christian Dallam Caswell, raised their children at the family plantation, Mulberry Point.

As told by Joe A. Mobley in his work, *North Carolina Governor Richard Caswell: Founding Father and Revolutionary Hero*, in 1743, Caswell's father began experiencing health problems. Additionally, Joppa declined as a seaport, which had an adverse impact on the family finances. Caswell Jr. and his brother, William, moved to North Carolina to find work and

Richard Caswell

buy land, establishing a place where the rest of the family could join them. The pair, carrying a letter of recommendation from Maryland's governor, arrived in New Bern, North Carolina, in 1745. The rest of the family soon joined them.

In New Bern, William became the deputy clerk of the Johnston County Court, while the 17-year-old Caswell became an apprentice to North Carolina's surveyor general. He would eventually become the deputy surveyor general, and he also acquired a small plantation. Caswell's family joined him there, and when his father died in 1755, he was buried on the property.

In 1754, Caswell was elected to the Colonial Assembly, where he would continue to serve until the American Revolution. By this time, he had married Mary Mackilwean, and the couple had three children, although their only son alone survived to adulthood, and Caswell's wife passed away due to complications from childbirth. Caswell would marry again in 1758 when he wed Sarah Herritage, who was the daughter of William Herritage, who was mentoring Caswell in the study of law. This second marriage would produce eight children, seven of whom survived to adulthood. In 1759, Caswell was admitted to the bar and began serving as the deputy attorney general while continuing to work in the Colonial Assembly.

As a member of the Assembly, Caswell was an active and influential figure, making numerous important contributions. He introduced bills aimed at increasing trade and commerce. He supported public welfare reforms, including providing a speedier release for those in debtor's prison. He championed both public education and court reform. Among his proposals was establishing a free school in every county using funds the colony had received for service during the French and Indian War.

On May 16th, 1771, Caswell commanded the right wing of the colonial governors' forces at the Battle of Alamance during the Regulator Insurrection in North Carolina. The conflict took place from 1766 to 1771, during which citizens took up arms against what they viewed as corrupt colonial officials. They were motivated by economic concerns, wanting a system that provided better economic conditions for more than just the colonial officials and plantation owners. On the day of the battle, Governor Tyson's militia numbered approximately 1,000 men. They faced a force twice that size. The Regulators were not a standing army but hoped that a show of force would result in the governor giving in to their demands. Tyson ordered the Regulators to disperse and waited an hour with no results. He then opened fire with cannons and muskets. When the smoke cleared, the Regulators had lost 100 killed and 200 wounded. Tyson's forces lost 9 men. Tyson followed the battle by conducting a terror campaign where he burned homes, hanged Regulators, and forced others to take loyalty oaths.

In 1774, Caswell was elected along with William Hooper and Joseph Hewes to represent North Carolina at the First Continental Congress. As told by Mobley in his Caswell biography, North Carolina's Governor Josiah Martin, who opposed the gathering, was initially pleased that Caswell had been elected. The governor wrote to the Earl of Dartmouth that "Richard Caswell has been appointed a delegate to the Continental Congress, but he disapproves of these measures in his heart, I am persuaded, and undertakes this office purely for the sake of maintaining his popularity on which he depends for continuance in the Treasureship which he has ever shown the best disposition to employ for the advantage of the government." Within one year that Governor's opinion changed dramatically saying of Caswell "he now shows himself to be the most active tool of sedition."

Caswell took his seat in Congress on September 17th. The evening before, he and his son, William, attended a banquet held to honor members of Congress. During the course of the celebration, 32 toasts were offered. Some of these noted loyalty to the mother country and the hope for reconciliation. Others declared an opposition to tyranny and support for Boston. Before Congress adjourned, it approved the Continental Association, which prohibited all trade with England. In addition, it authorized the formation of Committees of Safety to enforce the boycott, as well as the establishment of militias. Caswell affixed his signature to the measure.

Caswell, Hooper, and Hewes returned to Philadelphia to represent North Carolina in the Second Continental Congress. Some historians have noted that Caswell received no significant committee assignments and question whether this contributed to his decision to leave Congress on June 28th. According to Mobley, his actual motivation to leave Philadelphia was to "undertake the task of organizing North Carolina's Third Provincial Congress. That body approved the actions of the Continental Congress and raised two regiments for the new Continental Army. The Provincial Congress also elected Caswell, Hooper, and Hewes to serve in the Continental Congress for another year. Caswell was also appointed treasurer of the Southern District of North Carolina. Maintaining that he could not do both jobs, he resigned from Congress.

Caswell was the president of the North Carolina Provincial Congress, which, in 1776, drafted the first Constitution of North Carolina. That Congress elected him acting governor. He would be reelected and serve three terms, which was the maximum permitted by the new constitution. During his tenure, he oversaw issues related to the revolution, including raising troops, acquiring arms, and securing provisions. When he stepped down in 1780, he took over command of the militia and state troops.

Richard Caswell (1729–1789)

Grave of Richard Caswell

Inscription on top of headstone of Caswell's grave

In 1780, at the Battle of Camden Court House, the troops under his command fled after the Virginia militia broke, leaving him exposed to a British attack. The battle was a major victory for the English. After this defeat, Caswell returned to his home with an unnamed illness. Meanwhile, the North Carolina General Assembly appointed William Smallwood of Maryland to command the North Carolina militia without informing Caswell, and as a result, he resigned from his position. In 1781, Smallwood returned to Maryland, and Caswell was again appointed Major General of the Militia. He would serve in this position until the end of the American Revolution.

After the Revolution, Caswell served as state comptroller in 1782. He was a member and later served as President of the North Carolina State Senate from 1782 to 1784. He was once again elected governor in 1785. In 1787, he was appointed to be a delegate to the Constitutional Convention, but he did not attend. His final political position was as speaker of the North Carolina House of Commons. He passed away on November 10th, 1789, and was laid to rest in the Caswell Memorial Cemetery.

William Blount
(1749–1800)

Founder of Tennessee

Buried at First Presbyterian Church Cemetery,
Knoxville, Tennessee.

U.S. Constitution • First Governor Southwest Territory

William Blount was a signer of the Constitution, the only governor of the Southwest Territory which shortly became the state of Tennessee, and one of the first two Senators from Tennessee. He played a leading role in forming that state but was embroiled in an international conspiracy that ruined his reputation on the national level. However, Blount always remained popular in his home state.

Born on Easter Sunday, March 26, 1749, to Jacob Blount and Barbara Gray Blount, he was the eldest child of well-to-do plantation owners at "Rosefield" near Windsor, Bertie County, North Carolina. Soon after, Jacob Blount built the plantation "Blount Hall," in Pitt County, North Carolina. William was a descendant of Captain James Blount of Albermarle County, North Carolina, who was one of the leaders of Culpeper's Rebellion in 1677. He was also a descendant of King John of England and related to Lady Elizabeth Blount who bore an illegitimate son with King Henry VIII.

Blount's mother, Barbara Gray, was the daughter of the owner of "Rosefield," Scottish businessman John Gray. Jacob and Barbara had

Portrait of William Blount (circa 1828–1884) by Washington Bogart Cooper.

six more children after William: Anne, John Gray, Louisa, Reading, Thomas, and Jacob. Following Barbara Gray's premature death, Jacob married Hannah Salter, and they had five children, though only Willie and Sharpe lived to adulthood.

The Blount children were not formally educated, but the sons gained experience managing their father's plantation. Jacob taught his sons the profit potential of land speculation while raising livestock, cotton, and tobacco.

In the late 1760s and early 1770s, the Blount family was loyal to North Carolina Governor William Tryon. Jacob, a justice of the peace, provided supplies for Tryon's army prior to the Battle of Alamance in 1771. William, Jacob, and John Gray marched in Tryon's army. Many early historians called this battle the first of the American Revolution, though this point of view has faded in more recent times because the uprising was not an attempt to gain independence from the king, but rather to protest local corruption.

As tensions increased with England, the Blounts became patriots. Early in the Revolution, father Jacob and William were regimental paymasters for different militia districts in North Carolina. While not an officer, William was paid as if he were a captain. The family also contributed provisions to the cause. William was with George Washington in 1777 at the defense of Philadelphia and later helped defend Charleston against the British siege in 1780.

In 1778, William married Mary Grainier (Granger). The couple had six children; Ann, Mary Louisa, William Grainger, Richard Blackledge, Barbara, and Eliza.

William began running for a state House of Commons seat in 1779 but lost to Richard Dobbs Spaight in a contested election after a bitter battle. Eventually, the election results were voided due to proof of fraud. Meanwhile, in 1780, Blount was the official commissary to General Horatio Gates who oversaw the southern colonial forces. Blount was present when Gates lost the Battle of Camden in August of that year. Over $300,000 of soldier's pay was lost in the confusion of battle.

Blount ran again for the House of Commons seat in 1781 and won. In 1782, he was elected as one of North Carolina's four delegates to the Continental Congress. There he helped defeat new taxes and was for a strong army. He also introduced a bill known as the "Land Grab Act," which opened North Carolina's lands west of the Appalachians to settlement. Many soldiers used their grants to acquire land in this Tennessee Valley, or they sold them to the Blounts or other speculators. In 1784, Blount sponsored a bill that established the city of Nashville. He also sponsored a bill offering these lands to the Continental Congress to pay off North Carolina's war debts. While this narrowly passed, opponents repealed the act later in the year. However, in the meantime, a movement to establish the State of Franklin was underway led by John Sevier.

In 1785 and 1786, he worked to prevent the Hopewell Treaty that granted the Indians sizeable lands North Carolina speculators were hoping to retain. In 1787, Blount was a candidate for president of the

Congress but lost to Arthur St. Clair. In March of that year, Blount was one of five delegates from North Carolina to the Constitutional Convention in Philadelphia. He joined the convention in June, after it had started, and went back and forth between the Continental Congress and the convention, returning for final debates. Gouverneur Morris convinced Blount to sign the Constitution. Confident it was better for North Carolina, he then campaigned for its ratification in his home state which occurred in 1789.

Though Blount lost his race for Senate from North Carolina in November 1789, he continued to work on the creation of the Southwest Territory which included the so-called State of Franklin. In 1790, the Southwest Territory was formally created and President George Washington appointed William Blount as governor. William was sworn in at "Mount Vernon." Blount then went about organizing the territory. In 1791, he began construction of his mansion in the new city of Knoxville. He also negotiated the Treaty of Holston that year which brought thousands of acres of Indian lands under U.S. control. Despite the treaty, tensions continued with the Indians and western settlers.

The mansion of William Blount in downtown Knoxville, Tennessee (photo by Lawrence Knorr).

Blount then began implementing the steps required for statehood. This was achieved in early 1796. Blount realized he would lose an election to be the first governor to Sevier so he sought one of the two Senate seats from the new state. He was successful and represented the new state of Tennessee in Washington, D.C., when it was accepted into the union on May 31, 1796.

Meanwhile, during the early years of the republic, the Blount brothers had been accumulating lands in the west, amounting to over 2.5 million acres by the time he took his seat in the Senate. When land prices collapsed in 1795 following France's defeat of Spain in the War of the Pyrenees, the family went deeply into debt. William and his family attempted to sell lands to English investors but failed. Many feared the French would gain control of Louisiana and shut off American access to the Mississippi River.

To counter this, and to try to preserve his land values, Blount worked behind the scenes to convince the British to attack and take control of Florida and Louisiana. Blount's secret activities were betrayed when a letter spelling out the conspiracy made its way up the chain to President John Adams in early 1797. Adams sent the letter to the Senate where it was presented on July 3, 1797, while William was out. When he returned, the clerk read the letter aloud to Blount's stunned silence. Vice President Thomas Jefferson, who was sitting in the Senate, questioned Blount about the veracity of the letter, but Blount stammered for a postponement. This was granted.

William did not return the next day, but sent his fellow senator from Tennessee, William Cocke, to request more time again. This was rejected, and the Senate began an investigation. Blount tried to flee but was seized and testified before the committee, denying he wrote the letter. On July 8, the House of Representatives voted to hold impeachment hearings and the Senate voted 25 to 1 to sequester Blount's seat, effectively booting him from the body.

Blount left for home. The rest of the conspiracy came to light over the ensuing months. In early 1798, during Blount's impeachment hearing, a brawl erupted between congressman Matthew Lyon (Vermont) and Roger Griswold (Connecticut). On January 11, 1799, the Senate voted to dismiss the impeachment, arguing that such actions from the House do not affect Senators.

The "Blount Conspiracy" destroyed William's reputation and touched off a series of accusations between Federalists and Anti-federalists. George Washington hoped Blount would be "held in detestation by all good men." Abigail Adams called the conspiracy a "diabolical plot," and bemoaned the fact that there was no guillotine in Philadelphia. Others suggested the conspiracy was part of a greater French plot orchestrated by Thomas Jefferson or that it was an attempt to blackmail Spain.

While William was finished at the national level, he remained popular in his new home state of Tennessee where he was given a hero's welcome in September 1797. He became involved with the state Senate and was named Speaker in late 1798.

The worn slab covering the grave of William Blount. (photo by Lawrence Knorr).

William Blount (1749–1800)

In March 1800, an epidemic hit the area. While William tended to his family, he also fell ill on March 11. He died on the night of March 21, 1800, and is buried at the First Presbyterian Church Cemetery a short distance from his Knoxville home.

Blount County, Tennessee is named after William and several towns, forts, schools, and streets are named after him, his wife, or other family members. Blount Mansion still stands in downtown Knoxville and provides a museum dedicated to the Blount family. Blount is also honored by a bronze statue in the "Signers' Hall" exhibit at the National Constitution Center in Philadelphia and by a plaque on the first-floor rotunda of the North Carolina State Capitol.

Brother Thomas Blount represented North Carolina in the U.S. House of Representatives in the 1790s and 1800s. Half-brother Willie Blount was Governor of Tennessee from 1809 to 1815. The Blount children remained in politics or married prominently. William Grainger Blount represented Tennessee in the U.S. House of Representatives from 1815 to 1819. Mary Louisa Blount married Congressman Pleasant Miller, and Barbara Blount married General Edmund P. Gaines.

Thomas Burke
(1747–1783)

States' Rights Congressman

Buried at Governor Burke Gravesite,
Hillsborough, North Carolina.

Continental Congress • Governor

Thomas Burke was a physician and lawyer of Irish descent who lived in Hillsborough, North Carolina. He was a delegate to the Continental Congress and served as the third governor of North Carolina.

Burke was born circa 1747, in Tiaquin, County Galway, Ireland, the son of Ulick Burke and Leticia (née Ould) Burke, the sister of Sir Fielding Ould, a well-known physician. Both parents were Protestants.

As a youth, Burke lost his sight in his left eye and was also scarred by smallpox. He received some training in medicine, likely from his uncle, but the family was impoverished, and he was unable to complete his studies.

Burke emigrated to America when he was about fifteen years old. By 1764, he had relocated to Virginia, where he completed his medical studies and established a medical practice. However, he was unable to earn a living and began to study law. He also began to write about political matters, such as the Stamp Act, in the *Virginia Gazette*.

Burke was admitted to the Virginia colonial bar and established a law practice in Norfolk. It was here that he met a teacher named Mary

Thomas Burke (1747–1783)

Thomas Burke

Freeman. The two were married in March 1770. Not long after, their only child, a daughter named Polly, was born.

In 1772, now experiencing financial success, Burke moved his family to Hillsborough, North Carolina. He purchased a large estate and dubbed it Tyaquin, after his hometown. He opened a law practice there.

In 1775, Burke was elected to the first of four provincial congresses held at New Bern, Hillsborough, and Halifax. These continued into 1776, when, on April 12, he was part of a committee with Cornelius Harnett, Allen Jones, Abner Nash, John Kinchen, Thomas Person, and Thomas Jones, who penned what became known as the "Halifax Resolves," which illustrated North Carolina's protest against the king.

On December 20, 1776, Burke was appointed to the Continental Congress, arriving in Philadelphia on February 4, 1777. He attended sessions from February 4, 1777, until about September 10, 1777. Rather than fleeing with the Congress as the British invaded, Burke joined with General Nash's North Carolina troops to defend the city and was then at the Battle of Brandywine on September 11. Burke rejoined the Congress at Lancaster on September 27, and then at York from September 30 until

October 14, 1777. Burke was deeply involved in the formulation of the Articles of Confederation and consistently prioritized the rights of the states. Wrote one historian, "Burke took a most active part in framing those articles, and wrote repeated letters to Governor Richard Caswell, of his State, detailing the course of events. They are all of one tone and show a great jealousy of giving to Congress any powers that could possibly be retained by the States. Burke impressed upon Congress all through his career the necessity for guarding against any encroachment upon the power and dignity of the State . . . at one time, when standing out for what he thought were the prerogatives of the State, and desiring that a question under discussion be postponed for a day he threatened to secede unless his views were agreed to."

Burke served in the Continental Congress until 1781. He was known to be irascible at times, refusing to attend sessions during which matters he disagreed with were discussed, sometimes leaving Congress without a quorum. When threatened with arrest if he did not take his seat, Burke instead left and was seen as a folk hero back home. Wrote Congressman Thomas Rodney of Delaware on March 8, 1781:

> Doctr. Burk [sic], of N. Carolina, tho[ugh] not equal To Many Who have been in Congress, May Justly be Stiled [sic] the ablest And Most useful Member there at present. He has been in Congress five Years, is very Attentive and well Acquainted with business-is Nervous tho[ugh] Not Eloquent in his language, he is Correct and pointed in his debates, possesses the Honest integrity of a republican and is for preserving inviolable the rights of the people Without being lured away by power. Yet he is Some times not fully guarded from Dictatorial language and does not Attend Sufficiently To System, order and Arrangement, in a general view but Confines himself Too Much To particular Objects.

In June 1781, the North Carolina Assembly elected Burke as the third governor of North Carolina. He left the Continental Congress to assume his new role.

During the summer of 1781 in North Carolina, the Continental Army and militia were engaged in active combat against British troops and Loyalists. On September 12, Loyalists led by David Fanning raided the state legislature at Hillsborough and rounded up 200 Patriots, including Governor Burke. Burke was taken to Charleston, then Sullivan's Island, and finally, James Island. During this time, Patriots under the command of John Butler attempted a rescue but failed at the Battle of Lindley's Mill.

On James Island, Burke was paroled to live freely, but the conditions were deplorable, and he was mistreated. On January 16, 1782, he broke his parole agreement by escaping back to North Carolina. He wrote to the British authorities that he still considered himself under the terms of his parole, but he resumed his governor duties before he was properly exchanged. Many considered his behavior dishonorable. In April 1782, the North Carolina Assembly appointed Alexander Martin to succeed him.

In bad health and broken spirit, Burke returned to Tyaquin. There, ashamed, his wife took their daughter and left him. Burke died on December 2, 1783, at only thirty-six years of age. He was buried on his plantation near Hillsborough. His gravesite is about 350 feet north of Governor Burke Road.

Burke County, North Carolina, was named in his honor.

Cornelius Harnett
(1723 – 1781)

Hero of Cape Fear

Buried at St. James' Churchyard,
Wilmington, North Carolina.

Articles of Confederation

Cornelius Harnett was a wealthy plantation owner and merchant from Wilmington, North Carolina, who was also a Continental Congressman. He was a signer of the Articles of Confederation and died soon after being captured and tortured by the British.

Harnett was born in Edenton, Chowan County, North Carolina, on April 20, 1723. He was the son Cornelius Harnett, Senior, and his wife Elizabeth. The elder Harnett, a native of Ireland, was a colonial official and planter. In 1726, when young Cornelius was three, the family moved to Brunswick Town near what is now Cape Fear, close to the city of Wilmington, North Carolina. In that city, the younger Harnett grew to become a merchant and operated distilleries, businesses, and a schooner in the Cape Fear area. With the proceeds, he purchased a plantation called "Poplar Grove" nearby.

Meanwhile, Brunswick Town had become the busiest port in North Carolina, shipping goods to and from Europe and the British West Indies. When Spanish privateers attacked the first week of September 1748, the townspeople fled to the woods and their homes were looted. A local

Cornelius Harnett (1723–1781)

Etching of "Poplar Grove," the home of Cornelius Harnett near Wilmington, North Carolina.

captain, William Dry, rallied 67 men to expel the invaders. Among them was Cornelius Harnett, Jr. The counterattack was successful. Only one local was killed while ten privateers were killed and thirty captured. One of their two ships exploded, killing most aboard. The second ship was captured and the goods and slaves recovered. The contraband that was captured was subsequently sold to fund St. Philip's Church in Brunswick Town and St. James' Church in Wilmington.

In 1750, Harnett was elected as a member of the Wilmington city commission and appointed as a justice of the peace, where he served until 1777. In 1754, Harnett was elected to a seat in the North Carolina General Assembly. He took a leading role in that body following the passage of the Stamp Act by the British Parliament. Harnett joined in the march in Brunswick Town in February 1766 to openly protest the act. He became a leading voice against the royal governor, William Tryon, and became chairman of the local Sons of Liberty. In June 1770, Harnett led the resistance to the Townshend Acts, effectively boycotting British imports.

In December 1773, following the Boston Tea Party, Harnett joined the first Committee of Correspondence in North Carolina. He subsequently joined the North Carolina Council of Safety in 1776 as war with Britain was underway. Harnett was unanimously elected the group's president, becoming North Carolina's first (unelected) chief executive as an independent state. In this role, Harnett corresponded with political and military leaders. He also personally took up arms against the British, marching with General John Ashe to sack the British encampment at Fort Johnson. This drew the attention of the British who put a bounty on his head.

In 1776, Harnett served in the North Carolina provincial congresses in Halifax, North Carolina, and was chairman of the committee that drafted the state constitution. Under his direction, the group sent a document to the Continental Congress, now known as the "Halifax Resolves," calling for a declaration of independence from England. This was the first official action by a colony that called for separation from England.

Harnett was elected to the Continental Congress in May of 1777, just in time for Congress to abandon Philadelphia after the British occupation. Later that year, Harnett participated in the formulation of the Articles of Confederation to which he was a signer. Harnett returned to North Carolina at great risk at a time when the British were reasserting control throughout the south.

In January 1781, the British took Wilmington, North Carolina. Harnett, who was suffering from gout, was recuperating at a friend's house thirty miles away. He was found and captured by British Major James Craig's marauders. His hands and feet were tied and he

Grave of Cornelius Harnett at St. James Churchyard Cemetery in Wilmington, North Carolina (photo by Lawrence Knorr).

was tossed across a horse "like a sack of meal." Harnett was carried back to town where he was thrown in a blockhouse that had no roof. Exposed to the elements, Cornelius succumbed on April 18, 1781.

Harnett was laid to rest in St. James' Churchyard in Wilmington, North Carolina. He has a nondescript stone stating an incorrect date of death. Harnett County, North Carolina, is named in his honor. Harnett had married Mary Holt, but the couple had no children. She died in 1792.

Joseph Hewes
(1730 – 1779)

First Secretary of Naval Affairs

Buried at Christ Church Burial Ground,
Philadelphia, Pennsylvania.

Continental Association • Declaration of Independence

This founder was born in New Jersey but made his mark representing the state of North Carolina. He was raised by his Quaker parents. He attended Princeton College. He then decided to go into business and moved to Philadelphia to serve as an apprentice to the successful merchant and importer Joseph Ogden. He learned enough to become a very successful merchant on his own. Already an established businessman by the age of thirty, he relocated to North Carolina. It was in his adopted state that he made a name for himself politically when he was elected to the first Continental Congress in 1774. He was still in Congress when that body declared American independence and he proudly signed the document authored by Thomas Jefferson. He is also credited with playing a leading role in the creation of the Continental Navy and many consider him the first Secretary of the Navy. His name was Joseph Hewes.

Hewes was born on January 23, 1730, in Kingston, New Jersey. There is no dispute as to the fact that he attended Princeton College. What is in dispute is whether or not he graduated. Diploma or not, he was determined to make his way in the world of business. He worked initially as an apprentice in Philadelphia before establishing his own

Joseph Hewes (1730 – 1779)

Joseph Hewes

successful business. In 1760 at the age of thirty, he moved to Edenton, North Carolina which was a growing seaport on the Albemarle Sound. He successfully built a thriving business there as well but, while his professional life produced prosperity, his personal life produced heartbreak. Hewes was engaged to be married to the love of his life, Isabella Johnston, who died just days before their planned wedding. He would never marry.

Hewes was active in North Carolina's political affairs and was elected to the state legislature just three years after he settled there. Though he was an advocate for the rights of the colonies, he did not hold the view that separation from the mother country was best for America. It was a position he would champion up to the day Congress passed the motion declaring America's independence.

In 1774, North Carolina elected Hewes to the First Continental Congress. As a member of Congress, he supported measures that would harm his business interests. He strongly supported and worked to establish a nonimportation association. Since much of his own business dealings involved British imports, this action cost him dearly from a financial standpoint. But money was not all this patriot sacrificed for his country.

In 1775, the Quakers held a convention which denounced the Congress of which Hewes was a member. They announced that they opposed both war and the committees of Congress formed to aid in the American effort. Hewes responded by ending his affiliation with the Quakers siding with his nation against the religious beliefs of his parents.

Hewes was noted for being a hard and tireless worker in Congress. It appears that he applied the same energy, resolve, and determination he had used to build his business in his role as a representative of his state. Absenteeism was a major problem in Congress. By the fall of 1775, often more than 30% of the delegates were missing when the delegates were called to order. Hewes seldom missed even a committee meeting. In the momentous month of July 1776, he described his work as "too severe" noting that he sometimes attended meetings for eleven to twelve hours at a stretch "without eating or drinking." His health suffered but he refused to lessen his workload writing that he "obstinately persisted in doing my duty to the best of my judgment and abilities, and attended Congress the whole time, one day excepted."

As the mood in Congress shifted toward declaring independence, Hewes remained convinced that the colonies could achieve their objectives without separating from England. Though he still hoped for reconciliation with the mother country, he put his ships at the nation's disposal. He also used his influence to push hard to get a navy commander's assignment for a friend of his by the name of John Paul Jones. Hewes worked on a committee to rig the first navy ship and served as Secretary of the Naval Affairs Committee. Though he is in competition for the title with his friend Jones, many believe that it is Hewes who deserves to be called the "Father of the Navy."

When Richard Henry Lee introduced his resolution to declare independence in June of 1776, Hewes still felt that the action was premature. It was through the efforts of John Adams that Hewes was finally convinced to vote for independence. Adams would later recall "the unanimity of the States finally depended upon the vote of Joseph Hewes, and was finally determined by him." As for Hewes himself, after the resolution was adopted he lifted both hands and called out, "It is done! And I will abide by it."

In 1779, Hewes was still hard at work in Congress. He grew ill, probably as a result of overwork and undernourishment. Keeping his shoulder to the plow, he wrote, "My country is entitled to my services, and I shall not shrink from her cause, even though it should cost me my life." It did. Too ill to travel home to North Carolina, he died on October 10, 1779, at the age of 49. He was laid to rest in the Christ Church Burial Ground and his fellow congressmen wore a black crape around their arms for a month in his memory.

In 1894, an effort was made to move Hewes' remains back to North Carolina. On May 24th of that year, the *Wilmington Messenger* reported that his grave was lost. The paper noted that Hewes had been buried in the cemetery of Christ Episcopal Church in Philadelphia but that a "patient search failed to find either the grave or any record of it on the archives of the church." In 2003, the Christ Church Preservation Society published a small book written by Jean K. Wolf titled *Lives of the Silent Stones in the Christ Church Burial Ground*. In it, the author explains that the cemetery contains a donated commemorative plaque honoring Hewes because "the 1864 inscription book lists no grave marker for Joseph Hewes." Thus the burial site of this patriot and significant founder is unmarked.

The grave of Joseph Hewes

William Hooper
(1742–1790)

A Tory in the Continental Congress

Buried at Hillsborough Old Town Cemetery,
Hillsborough, North Carolina.
Partially reinterred at Guilford Courthouse National Military Park,
Greensboro, North Carolina.

Continental Association • Declaration of Independence

Like many Americans at the time, William Hooper saw no compelling reason to support a revolution and break with England. He came from an environment of privilege and was a successful lawyer and politician in North Carolina. While serving in the North Carolina General Assembly, his support for the colonial government began to erode. He slowly became a supporter of the American Revolution and independence, served as a delegate in both Continental Congresses, and signed the Declaration of Independence.

William Hooper was born in Boston on June 28, 1742, the first of five children born to William Hooper and Mary Dennie. His father was a Scottish minister who studied at the University of Edinburgh before immigrating to Boston. Valuing education, the father saw that young William received a grand education for the times, attending the prestigious Boston Latin School and in 1757 entering Harvard College. Three years later, at the age of eighteen, he was awarded a bachelor of

William Hooper (1742–1790)

William Hooper

arts degree. Three years after that, he was granted a master's degree in theology, but much to his parent's disappointment, he refused to enter the clergy and instead chose to study law under James Otis, one of Massachusetts's leading attorneys. Many biographies have stated that Otis's passionate stands for colonial rights influenced the young Hooper. He studied under Otis until 1764 when he passed the bar exam and left Massachusetts for Wilmington, North Carolina. He became the circuit lawyer for Cape Fear and became very popular and respected by the planters and lawyers. By June 1766, he was unanimously elected Recorder of the Borough.

In August 1767, Hooper married Anne Clark, a North Carolina native and daughter of the sheriff of New Hanover County. The couple would have two sons and a daughter.

In 1769 the North Carolina Governor William Tryon named Hooper the Deputy Attorney General of the Salisbury district and the following year named him Deputy Attorney General for the entire colony. It was during this time that Hooper came in conflict with a group called the "Regulators." These farmers opposed excessive colonial government taxation, excessive legal fees, and the corruption of the royal government's officers. They took up arms and rioted to show their bitterness. In 1770, a group of Regulators reportedly dragged Hooper through the streets in a riot in Hillsborough. Hooper urged the governor to use force to end this rebellion. The governor took his advice, and at what became known as the Battle of Alamance in May 1771, routed the Regulators, and the movement was destroyed. It is considered by some to be the opening salvo of the American Revolution. At that point, it certainly appeared that Hooper was a firm supporter of the royal government.

Things started to change when in 1773, Hooper was elected to the North Carolina legislature. He became an opponent of a bill pushed by the colonial governor that would regulate the court system. He wrote a series of essays that he anonymously signed as "Hampden." Although now lost to history, it was one of the first times media was used to oppose proposed legislation. The outcome was that most of the provincial courts were closed and that Hooper, once his authorship became known, was disbarred from practicing law for one year. This episode soured his reputation among loyalists.

During his time in the Assembly, Hooper slowly became a supporter of the American Revolution and independence from Britain. The governor soon disbanded the Assembly, and Hooper helped organize a new colonial assembly without the Royal Government's consent. His loyalist father was so displeased he disowned his son.

In early 1774 Hooper was one of the leaders of the anti-British agitation in North Carolina. He was appointed to the Committee of Correspondence and Inquiry to coordinate activities with other colonies. In June of 1774, the port of Boston was closed by the British, and Hooper took the lead in mustering aid and support for his native city. Two shiploads of provisions and 2000 pounds in currency were sent for relief. Later that year, he was chosen as one of the delegates to the First Continental Congress. Some delegates, including Thomas Jefferson, believing that he still harbored loyalty to the Crown, referred to Hooper as the "Tory in the Continental Congress." He served diligently on numerous committees and was elected to the Second Continental Congress. There he served honorably in the assembly where Jefferson drafted the Declaration of Independence. Much of his time was split between Congress and working on forming a new government in North Carolina. Due to this, he missed the vote approving the Declaration of Independence on July 4, 1776; however, he arrived in time to sign it on August 2, 1776. He was the youngest signer at 34.

In 1777 due to financial difficulties, Hooper resigned from Congress and returned to North Carolina to resume his law career. Throughout the revolution, he was sought by the British as a traitor for signing the Declaration of Independence. They targeted him to show others the consequences of his actions. In 1780 the British invaded North Carolina. Hooper moved his family from Finian, his country home, into Wilmington for safety, but in January 1781, while he was away, Wilmington fell to the enemy, and Hooper was separated from his family. The British burned his estates in Finian and Wilmington, forcing Hooper to rely on friends for food and shelter and nursing him back to health after contracting malaria. His wife Anne and his children were forced to flee to Hillsborough, where her brother found shelter. After

William Hooper's monument.

nearly a year of separation, Hooper was reunited with his family, and they settled in Hillsborough, where he continued to work with the North Carolina assembly until 1783.

After the war, Hooper's popularity waned as he was lenient towards loyalists. In 1787 and 1788, he campaigned heavily to ratify the new United States Constitution, although he refused election to the convention that ultimately ratified the document. He was appointed a federal judge in 1789 and served for one year before his bad health forced him to retire. His recurrences of malaria and his alcoholism contributed to his death on October 14, 1790, at 48. He was quietly buried in the garden of his estate, which later became a part of the Old Town Cemetery in Hillsborough. Later, in 1894 his remains were reportedly reinterred in the Guilford Courthouse National Military Park in Greensboro, North Carolina, where a huge marker was placed over his grave. Many historians believe that much of his remains are still in his original grave. His home in Hillsborough was declared a National Historic Landmark in 1971.

James Iredell
(1751–1799)

An Original Supreme

Buried at Hayes Plantation Cemetery, aka Johnston Family Cemetery, Edenton, North Carolina.

First Supreme Court

James Iredell, of North Carolina, was an English-born lawyer and political essayist who was appointed to the first US Supreme Court by President George Washington. He was a leading Federalist in the state and the father of a governor of North Carolina, James Iredell Jr.

Iredell was born on October 5, 1751, in Lewes, England, the son of Francis Iredell, a merchant in Bristol, and his wife, Margaret (née McCulloch) Iredell, of Dublin, Ireland. Iredell was the oldest of five surviving children. Circa 1768, due to his father's business failure, young James, at age 17, sailed to America to become the Comptroller of Customs for King George III in the village of Edenton, North Carolina. The position had been arranged by relatives. This also provided the funds and opportunity to study law under Samuel Johnston, who later became a governor of North Carolina and a US Senator.

In 1771, Iredell was admitted to the North Carolina bar. Two years later, in 1773, he married Samuel Johnston's sister, Hannah. After twelve childless years, the couple ultimately had four children. In 1774, Iredell was made the tariff collector for the port.

James Iredell

Despite working for the crown, in 1774, Iredell wrote *To the Inhabitants of Great Britain*, challenging parliamentary supremacy over the colonies. At age 23, Iredell became the most influential political essayist in North Carolina. He followed this with *Principles of an American Whig*, laying out many of the themes that later appeared in the Declaration of Independence.

During the American Revolution, Iredell served North Carolina by helping to organize the court system as a member of the commission that drafted the initial court bill. He was elected a judge of the superior court in 1778, serving only to make one circuit to settle old lawsuits. He then filled numerous roles over the years, including the state's second attorney general from 1779 to 1781. He resigned soon after the surrender at Yorktown to return to his family to "repair the sufferings [his] poor circumstances had received in the public service."

In 1787, Iredell was appointed by the state assembly to lead a commission to compile and revise North Carolina's laws. This was later published in 1791 as *Iredell's Revisal*. As the new U.S. Constitution was being debated, Iredell was the first to support it in North Carolina. He responded in 1788, under the pseudonym "Marcus," to George Mason's eleven objections with what were later called *Iredell's Answers*. This preceded the more famous *Federalist Papers*. Ultimately, the Constitution did not pass in North Carolina, despite his efforts. Only after the Bill of Rights was passed did North Carolina affirm in 1789. Regardless, Iredell was lauded as the intellectual leader of the Federalists' victory.

As a reward for his efforts to ratify the Constitution, George Washington appointed Iredell to the first U.S. Supreme Court on February 8, 1790, as an associate justice. He was confirmed by the Senate two days later and sworn into office on May 12.

Grave of James Iredell

During his nearly decade on the bench, Iredell was an ardent Federalist, vigorously supporting the administrations of Washington and Adams. However, the court only met twice a year and made its first decision in 1791. Iredell was involved in two noteworthy decisions:

- *Chisholm v. Georgia* (1793): Concerning interstate lawsuits. Iredell's dissent led to the 11th Amendment.
- *Calder v. Bull* (1798): Concerning ex post facto laws.

During his tenure, Iredell also "rode the circuit" as did all the Supreme Court justices twice a year. Over the years, this travel proved very taxing. Iredell died at age 48 on October 20, 1799. He was buried in the Johnston family cemetery in Edenton, North Carolina.

Iredell County, North Carolina, and the SS *James Iredell*, a ship from World War II, were named in his honor. The James Iredell House in Edenton is on the National Register of Historic Places.

Iredell and his wife appeared as characters in the historical novel by Natalie Wexler titled *A More Obedient Wife: A Novel of the Early Supreme Court*.

John Penn
(1741–1788)

The Penn with a Pen

Buried at Guilford Courthouse National Military Park,
Greensboro, North Carolina.

Declaration of Independence • Articles of Confederation

Though born and raised in Virginia this Founder represented North Carolina in the Continental Congress. His chief contribution to the cause of American independence was affixing his name to the document that declared it. A skilled attorney he was noted for his oratorical gifts in his practice before judges and juries. He also reasoned his way out of a duel with the President of Congress as they were on their way to the dueling ground. His name was John Penn.

Penn was born on May 17, 1741, just outside of Fredericksburg, Virginia. His father was a farmer and his mother the daughter of a county judge. It appears that Penn's father did not value education as his son only attended school for a couple of years. By the time he reached the age of 18, Penn had different ideas regarding how to make his way in the world. His cousin, Edmund Pendleton, was an attorney and Penn began borrowing books from his library which he used to teach himself to read and write. Next, he studied law under Pendleton and earned his license to practice when he was 21.

Penn would practice the law for over a decade in Virginia. During that time he married Susan Lyme and the couple would welcome three

Portrait of John Penn etched by H B Hall from a drawing in the collection of Dr. F A Emmet, 1871.

children into the world. In 1774 the Penns moved to North Carolina where he not only resumed his law practice but also developed an interest in the patriot cause. He certainly impressed the people in his adopted state as in 1775 he was elected as a representative to the second Continental Congress.

It would seem that as a member of Congress, Penn was a strong supporter of American independence. Early in 1776, he wrote to Thomas Person, a brigadier general in the North Carolina militia. Penn urged Person to "encourage our people, animate them to dare to even die for their country. Our struggle I hope will not continue long, may unanimity and success crown your endeavours."

On July 2, 1776, Penn and the other North Carolina representative Joseph Hewes voted in favor of American independence. The duo along with a third representative from North Carolina, William Hooper, who had been absent the day of the vote, signed the Declaration on August 2nd.

John Penn (1741–1788)

In 1778 Penn added his signature to the Articles of Confederation. It was during this time period that Penn found himself in multiple political arguments with Henry Laurens from South Carolina who had succeeded John Hancock as the President of Congress. Their battles reached a boiling point, at least for Laurens, and he challenged Penn to a duel to settle their differences.

The two would-be duelists lived in the same boarding house. The morning they were to meet on the field of honor, they sat together to eat their breakfast. Upon completing their meal, they walked together to the site chosen for the duel. Along the way, they came to a large muddy spot they needed to cross. Penn, being the younger man, proceeded to help Laurens across. During the crossing, Penn offered to let the whole matter drop and Laurens quickly agreed. They exchanged apologies and canceled the duel.

Penn left Congress in 1780 and the Governor of North Carolina, Abner Nash, promptly appointed him to his state's Board of War. Penn was an active member of the board and worked to supply war materials to Nathanael Greene's Continentals and Francis Marion's guerrillas. When the Revolution ended, he served for a short period of time as North Carolina's receiver of taxes for the Confederation government. He resigned this post because, in his view, he had not been given the authority he required to collect the taxes. He then returned to the practice of law.

Grave of John Penn at Guilford Courthouse National Military Park in Greensboro, North Carolina (photo by Lawrence Knorr).

Penn passed away on September 14, 1788, at the age of 47. He was laid to rest on the grounds of his home. In 1894 Penn's unmarked grave was located in a pasture marked by two large sassafras trees. According to *The Wilmington Messenger* authorities were able to find Penn's skull as well as many pieces of the walnut coffin. As reported by that paper these "sacred remains" were placed in a copper box and buried on the Guilford Battle Ground beneath a monument erected to honor North Carolina's signers. That spot marks John Penn's final resting place.

Richard Dobbs Spaight
(1758–1802)

The Dueling Signer

Buried at Clermont Estate Cemetery,
New Bern, North Carolina.

Military • US Constitution

This founder was a successful politician and planter born and bred in his native state of North Carolina. He fought in the American Revolution. He represented his state in the Continental Congress from 1782 to 1785. He was one of the delegates chosen to represent North Carolina at the 1787 Constitutional Convention held in Philadelphia. He was also a signer of the document that gathering produced. He also served as governor of his state and in the United States House of Representatives. He would become the first of two signers of the Constitution to be killed in a duel. Similar to Alexander Hamilton, his opponent in the duel was a political rival. His name was Richard Dobbs Spaight.

As told by Denise Kiernan and Joseph D'Agnese in their work *Signing Their Rights Away,* Spaight was born on March 25, 1758, in the coastal town of New Bern, North Carolina. His mother was the sister of the royal governor, and his father was a wealthy planter. By the time he was eight, both his parents had died, and the orphan was sent to live with relatives in Northern Ireland. When the American Revolutionary War broke out, Spaight was attending the University of Glasgow. After he graduated, he returned to North Carolina.

Upon his arrival in America, Spaight served as an aide-de-camp to Major General Richard Caswell at the Battle of Camden, also known as

Richard Dobbs Spaight

the Battle of Camden Court House. The fighting took place on August 16, 1780, north of Camden, South Carolina. Lord Cornwallis commanded the British forces while the Americans were led by the American general who had defeated the British at Saratoga three years earlier. In his work, *Patriots*, A. J. Langguth writes that when Gates embarked on his first mission in the southern theater, his friend Charles Lee told him, "Take care lest your Northern laurels turn to Southern willows." Despite having a significant numerical superiority, the American forces were routed, and Gates never held a field command again.

After the Revolution, Spaight, armed with his considerable wealth and war record, entered politics. The North Carolina General Assembly elected him to serve in the Congress of Confederation between 1782 and 1785. Here, Spaight played a key role relative to the Land Ordinance of 1784. This ordinance called for the land in the recently created United States, located west of the Appalachian Mountains, north of the Ohio

River, and east of the Mississippi River, to be divided into separate states. Thomas Jefferson was the principal author of the proposal considered by Congress. One of the articles proposed by Jefferson was that after the year 1800, there shall be neither slavery nor involuntary servitude in any of the new states. Spaight, seconded by Jacob Read of South Carolina, moved to strike out this article. In a letter dated April 25, 1784, from Jefferson to James Madison, the future president wrote, "The clause was lost by one individual vote only." Jefferson blamed the defeat on Spaight and never forgave him, and would describe him as the man who permitted slavery to expand westward.

From 1785 to 1787, Spaight served in the North Carolina House of Commons, where he was named Speaker of the House. In 1787, he represented his state at the Constitutional Convention in Philadelphia. As noted by Clinton Rossiter in his work, *1787: The Grand Convention*, Spaight, at 29, was one of the youngest delegates to attend the gathering. Rossiter describes Spaight as somewhat of a straddler on critical issues who was thought to lean toward a more powerful federal government. To the best of our knowledge, he attended every session. In assessing Spaight's performance, Rossiter calls him "one of the usefuls who had several small triumphs as the plugger of holes." One example is that Spaight was successful in persuading the convention to give the President the power to make recess appointments. At the convention's conclusion, he added his signature to the Constitution.

In 1788, Spaight was a delegate to North Carolina's ratifying convention. He supported ratification, but the convention voted against ratification. In that same year, he married Mary Leach, who had the distinction of being the First Lady to dance with George Washington at a ball held in Washington's honor at the Governor's Palace, New Bern, in 1791.

Spaight retired from politics for several years, citing health reasons. He returned to public service in 1792, when he was elected to the state House of Representatives. That same year, the General Assembly elected him as the first native-born governor of North Carolina. He would be reelected for two further one-year terms. He moved the state capital to Raleigh and played a key role in the founding of the University of North Carolina at Chapel Hill.

Spaight was elected to the United States House of Representatives in 1798, filling the unexpired term of Nathan Bryan, who had passed away. A year later, he was elected to a two-year term. He tried for a second full term but lost to his Federalist opponent, John Stanly. Upon returning to North Carolina, Spaight served in the North Carolina Senate. Stanly began to criticize his predecessor, saying that Spaight wasn't sickly but used health as an excuse to avoid taking a position on controversial issues. The situation escalated, resulting in a duel. The duel took place at 5:30 in the afternoon on September 5, 1802, behind New Bern's Masonic Hall. Approximately three hundred people witnessed the event. The two men aimed and fired, but both missed their target. The men reloaded and fired again with the same result. Some of the townspeople implored the two to call a truce, but Spaight refused. The third shots also missed, but on the fourth attempt, Spaight was struck in the side and mortally wounded, and he died the next day. Stanly was charged with murder but pardoned by the governor.

Spaight was laid to rest in Clermont Cemetery in New Bern, North Carolina. There is a local legend saying that Union soldiers desecrated his grave during the Civil War. The authors believe this to be unlikely.

Duel between Spaight and John Stanly

Richard Dobbs Spaight (1758–1802)

Grave of Richard Dobbs Spaight

John Williams
(1731–1799)

North Carolina Speaker of the House

Buried at Montpelier Plantation Cemetery,
Henderson, North Carolina.

Articles of Confederation • Military • Judge

John Williams, of North Carolina, was a colonel in the North Carolina militia and a member of the North Carolina House of Commons, where he became speaker. He was also a land speculator, involved in the acquisition of Kentucky. As a member of the Continental Congress, he signed the Articles of Confederation. He was also a superior court judge during his later years and a founder of the University of North Carolina.

Williams was born on March 14, 1731, in Surry County, North Carolina, the son of John Williams, IV, a planter, and his wife, Mary (née Womack) Williams, of Granville County, Virginia. He studied law and established a practice near his North Carolina plantation with his cousin, Richard Henderson. On November 12, 1759, Williams married a widow named Agnes Keeling (née Bullock). They produced one daughter, Agatha.

In 1768, Williams was appointed Deputy Attorney General of North Carolina. He was also commissioned to the ceremonial position of colonel in the North Carolina militia. Meanwhile, his plantation, Montpelier, outside of the future Williamsborough, was one of the most substantial in Granville County.

John Williams (1731–1799)

John Williams

During the 1760s, cousins Williams and Henderson pursued land ventures. In 1769, they hired Daniel Boone to survey the land between the Cumberland and Kentucky Rivers. In August 1774, when founding the Louisa Company, Henderson employed Boone to "make contacts with influential Cherokees to learn their attitude toward the sale of some of their lands in the Kentucky area to white purchasers."

The following March, Henderson and Boone signed the Treaty of Sycamore Shoals, also known as the Treaty of Watauga, leading to the Transylvania Purchase from the Cherokees of "a tract of 20 million acres lying north of the Cumberland River, southeast of the Ohio River, and west of the Cumberland Mountains, with a narrow access route extending from Sycamore Shoals to Cumberland Gap."

Meanwhile, Williams was involved with the state legislature, representing Granville County. During the congress's meeting in Hillsborough from August 24 to September 10, 1775, the delegates reviewed an early draft of the "Articles of the Confederacy." During this time, on September 9, Williams was commissioned as a lieutenant colonel under Colonel James Thackston of the Orange County Minutemen Regiment.

Meanwhile, Williams was named a resident agent of Boonesborough, Kentucky, for the Transylvania Company on September 25, 1775. According to the company's minutes, he was "to transact their business in the said Colony; and he is accordingly invested with full power, by letter of Attorney. Mr. Williams shall proceed to Boonesborough, in the said Colony, as soon as possible, and continue there until the twelfth day of April next; and to be allowed, for his services, one hundred and fifty pounds, Proclamation money of North Carolina, out of the profits arising from the sale of lands, after discharging the Company's present engagements."

Pulled away from his land pursuits, Colonel Williams was at the Battle of Moore's Creek Bridge on February 27, 1776. The minutemen regiments were then disbanded on April 10, 1776. Williams continued as a colonel and commandant of the 9th North Carolina Regiment of the North Carolina Line from 1776 to 1778.

Williams was elected to the North Carolina House of Commons from 1777 to 1778 and was named Speaker of the House. In 1778, he was appointed to the Continental Congress and signed the Articles of Confederation in Philadelphia on July 21. However, Williams resigned from the Continental Congress on February 1, 1779, seeking to return home.

Upon his return to North Carolina in 1779, the village near his plantation was named Williamsborough in his honor. It served as the state's temporary capital during the skirmishes between Loyalists and the North Carolina militia, from the summer of 1781 to February 1782. It was formally incorporated in 1787.

Additionally, in 1779, Williams was appointed as a judge to the Court of Conference, which effectively served as the state's superior court. His most notable ruling was during *Bayard v. Singleton* in 1787, the first example of a court exercising judicial review in the United States. This case was widely published and was credited as setting a precedent for the US Supreme Court's *Marbury v. Madison*.

Williams served more than twelve years as a judge and then devoted the rest of his life to supporting education. He was one of the seven founding trustees of the University of North Carolina at Chapel Hill in 1792. Williams also donated many books to the library and an ostrich egg to the museum.

Williams died on October 10, 1799, and was buried in the family plot at his estate, Montpelier.

Hugh Williamson
(1735 – 1819)

"The Ben Franklin of North Carolina"

Buried at Trinity Church Cemetery,
New York, New York

US Constitution • First US Congress

Hugh Williamson was a Pennsylvania-born physician, scholar, and politician who was elected to the Continental Congress, where he signed the US Constitution on behalf of North Carolina. He lived in several states during his lifetime and was known as North Carolina's Benjamin Franklin.

Williamson, born December 5, 1735, in West Nottingham Township, Chester County, Pennsylvania, was the son of John Williamson, a clothier, and his wife, Mary (née Davison) Williamson. The Williamsons were devout Presbyterians of Scots-Irish descent. Apparently too frail for the family's clothier business, Williamson was encouraged to become a minister and was sent to Francis Alison's New London Academy near Newark, Delaware, graduating in 1754.

Upon graduation, Williamson spent the next three years studying mathematics at the College of Philadelphia, the predecessor of the University of Pennsylvania. He graduated in the school's first class on May 17, 1757, five days before his father died.

Over the next few years, as he settled his father's estate, he tutored Latin at the Philadelphia Academy and continued his theological studies

Hugh Williamson

with Reverend Samuel Finley, his neighbor in West Nottingham, who later became the president of the College of New Jersey. Williamson moved to Connecticut and obtained a preacher's license but was disillusioned by the divisions in the Presbyterian Church and burdened by ill health. He turned again to academics and completed a master's degree at the College of Philadelphia in 1760 and joined the faculty as a professor of mathematics.

However, Williamson continued to study and became interested in the human body and its functions. He studied medicine at the University of Edinburgh and the University of Utrecht in the Netherlands. He received his medical degree on August 6, 1764, and returned to Philadelphia to open a practice. A polymath, he also continued other scientific pursuits and projects, landing membership in the American Philosophical Society in 1768 and acclaim in Europe in intellectual circles for his work on the transits of Venus and Mercury and his papers "An Attempt to Account for the Change in Climate" and "An Essay on Comets." All contained original ideas, leading to an honorary doctorate from the University of Leyden in the Netherlands.

Hugh Williamson (1735–1819)

In 1773, to raise money for a new academy in Newark, Delaware, Williamson traveled to the West Indies and then to Europe, stopping in Boston in mid-December. There, he witnessed the Boston Tea Party on December 18, as Patriots disguised as Indians tossed crates of tea into the harbor in protest of Parliament's tax.

Upon reaching England a few weeks later, Williamson was summoned before the Privy Council to testify regarding the rebellion in Boston and colonial affairs generally. He warned the councilors that there would be further trouble if policies were not changed. At the time, he was collaborating with Benjamin Franklin in London on electrical experiments. Williamson published an anonymous "Plea of the Colonies," hoping to encourage sympathetic Whigs to side with the Americans. He also may have been involved in the controversy regarding Benjamin Franklin, the colonial postmaster, and the letters of Massachusetts Royal Governor Thomas Hutchinson which called for an abridgment of colonial rights. He stayed in England, in scientific circles, for a while before moving on to the Netherlands. He was there in July 1776 when the colonies declared independence.

Williamson returned to Philadelphia in early 1777 and volunteered as a doctor in the Continental Army. He thought his best contribution would be procuring medications, so he headed to Charleston, South Carolina, to open a business in partnership with his brother John. The goal was to obtain scarce items from the West Indies that would circumvent the British blockades.

Later, on his way to Baltimore, he was waylaid in Edenton, North Carolina, and decided to make his base of operations there. Williamson quickly became connected to the government in North Carolina, answering the call of Major General and Governor Richard Caswell to be the state's Physician and Surgeon General. Williamson accepted and held the post until the end of the Revolution.

By 1780, Williamson worked as a field surgeon, treating troops in South Carolina following the stunning defeat of American forces in Charleston. After the Battle of Camden, Williamson insisted on attending to victims on both sides of the conflict due to widespread smallpox. He then joined Major General Nathanael Greene's campaign to liberate the South.

After the war, Williamson was elected to the North Carolina House of Commons and the Continental Congress in 1782. He brought with him a Federalist perspective. In 1786, North Carolina selected Williamson to attend the Annapolis Convention but arrived too late to have an impact. The following year, he was appointed to the Constitutional Convention in Philadelphia. There, he lodged with Alexander Hamilton and James Madison and led the North Carolina delegation. Though personally opposed to slavery, Williamson voted for the "Three-Fifths Compromise" that permitted its continuance. Near the end of the convention, Williamson wrote what was known as the "Letters of Sylvius," urging North Carolina to ratify the Constitution. The decision was whether the United States would remain a "system of patchwork and a series of expedients" or become "the most flourishing, independent, and happy nation on the face of the earth." Thomas Jefferson summed up Williamson's contributions, noting he was "a very useful member, of an acute mind, attentive to business, and of a high degree of erudition."

After he signed the US Constitution, Williamson returned to the Congress in New York to wrap up. He then returned to North Carolina to urge its ratification, saying it was "more free and more perfect than any form of government that has ever been adopted by any nation."

Williamson was elected to the First Federal Congress and served two terms. He opposed the establishment of the Bank of the United States, the federal government's assumption of state debt, the whiskey excise tax, and the Jay Treaty.

Williamson finally married Maria Apthorpe, the daughter of Charles Ward Apthorpe, in January 1789. The couple had two sons, but Maria died during the birth of their second child in 1790. The child died soon after. Williamson decided not to run again for Congress and retired to New York City. There, he continued to write and research and raise his son, who perished in 1811 at the age of 22.

Over the years, Williamson published a wide range of works, including a two-volume *History of North Carolina* (1812). He advocated for inland canals, leading later to the Erie Canal. He was also a trustee or founding member of the University of North Carolina, the New York College of Physicians and Surgeons, and the New York Literary and Philosophical

Society. His philanthropy involved the support and development of an orphan asylum, the humane society, and a hospital dispensary. He was also a prominent member of the New York Historical Society, and in 1813, Williamson was elected to the American Antiquarian Society.

Williamson died suddenly in New York City on May 22, 1819, while driving his carriage. He was 83. He was buried in Trinity Churchyard in New York City, near the grave of Alexander Hamilton.

Williamson Counties in Tennessee and Illinois were named for him. Williamson Street in Madison, Wisconsin, also carries his name.

Grave of Hugh Williamson

Sources

Books, Magazines, Journals, Files:
Alexander, Edward P. *Revolutionary Conservative: James Duane of New York.* New York: Ams Press, 1978.
Anthony, Katharine Susan. *First Lady of the Revolution; The Life of Mercy Otis Warren.* Port Washington, N.Y.: Kennikat Press, 1972.
Appleby, Joyce. *Inheriting the Revolution: The First Generation of Americans.* Cambridge, Massachusetts: Harvard University Press, 2000.
Atkinson, Rick. *The British Are Coming: The War for America, Lexington to Princeton, 1775–1777.* New York: Henry Holt & Co. 2019.
Bordewich, Fergus M. *The First Congress: How James Madison, George Washington, and a Group of Extraordinary Men Invented the Government.* New York: Simon and Schuster Paperbacks, 2016.
Boudreau, George W. *Independence: A Guide to Historic Philadelphia.* Yardley, Pennsylvania: Westholme Publishing, LLC. 2012.
Bowen, Catherine Drinker. *Miracle at Philadelphia: The Story of the Constitutional Convention May to September 1787.* Boston, Massachusetts: Little, Brown & Company, 1966.
Breen, T.H, *George Washington's Journey: The President Forges a New Nation.* New York: Simon & Schuster. 2016.
Brookhiser, Richard. *Gentleman Revolutionary: Gouverneur Morris The Rake Who Wrote the Constitution.* New York: Free Press, 2003.
———. *John Marshall: The Man Who Made the Supreme Court.* New York: Basic Books. 2018.
Brush, Edward Hale. *Rufus King and His Times.* New York: N.L. Brown, 1926.
Chadwick, Bruce. I Am Murdered: *George Wythe, Thomas Jefferson, and the Killing That Shocked a New Nation.* Hoboken, New Jersey: John Wiley & Sons, 2009.
Chambers, II, John Whiteclay. *The Oxford Companion to American Military History.* Oxford: Oxford University Press, 1999.
Commager, Henry Steele & Richard B. Morris. *The Spirit of 'Seventy-Six: The Story of the American Revolution as Told by Participants.* New York: Harper & Rowe, 1967.
Cole, Ryan. *Light-Horse Harry Lee: The Rise and Fall of a Revolutionary Hero.* Washington, D.C.: Regnery History. 2019.
Conlin, Joseph R. *The Morrow Book of Quotations in American History.* New York: William Morrow and Company, Inc., 1984.
Daniels, Jonathan. *Ordeal of Ambition.* Garden City, New York: Doubleday & Company, Inc., 1970.
Dann, John C. *The Revolution Remembered: Eyewitness Accounts of the War for Independence.* Chicago: University of Chicago Press, 1980.

SOURCES

DeRose, Chris. *Founding Rivals: Madison vs. Monroe: The Bill of Rights and the Election that Saved a Nation*. New York: MJF Books, 2011.
Drury, Bob & Tom Clavin. *Valley Forge*. New York: Simon & Schuster. 2018.
Ellis, Joseph J. *Revolutionary Summer: The Birth of American Independence*. New York: Alfred A. Knopf, 2013.
———. *The Quartet: Orchestrating the Second American Revolution, 1783–1789*. New York: Alfred A. Knopf, 2015.
———. *His Excellency: George Washington*. New York: Alfred A. Knopf, 2004.
Flexner, James Thomas. *George Washington in the American Revolution, 1775–1783*. Boston: Little, Brown & Company, 1967.
Flower, Lenore Embick. "Visit of President George Washington to Carlisle, 1794." Carlisle, Pennsylvania: The Hamilton Library and Cumberland County Historical Society, 1932.
Gerlach, Don R. *Proud Patriot: Philip Schuyler and the War of Independence, 1775–1783*. Syracuse, N.Y.: Syracuse University Press, 1987.
Goodrich, Charles A. *Lives of the Signers of the Declaration of Independence*. Charlotteville, N.Y.: SamHar Press, 1976.
Griffith, IV, William R. *The Battle of Lake George: England's First Triumph in the French and Indian War*. Charleston, South Carolina: The History Press, 2016.
Grossman, Mark. *Encyclopedia of the Continental Congress*. Armenia, New York: Grey House Publishing, 2015.
Hamilton, Edward P. *Fort Ticonderoga: Key to a Continent*. Boston: Little, Brown & Company, 1964.
Isenberg, Nancy. *Fallen Founder: The Life of Aaron Burr*. New York: Penguin Group, 2007.
Kennedy, Roger G. *Burr, Hamilton, and Jefferson: A Study in Character*. New York: Oxford University Press, 1999.
Kiernan, Denise & Joseph D'Agnese. *Signing Their Lives Away: The Fame and Misfortune of the Men Who Signed the Declaration of Independence*. Philadelphia: Quirk Books, 2008.
———. *Signing Their Rights Away: The Fame and Misfortune of the Men Who Signed the United States Constitution*. Philadelphia: Quirk Books, 2011.
Klarman, Michael J. *The Framers' Coup: The Making of the United States Constitution*. New York: Oxford University Press, 2016.
Langguth, A. J. *Patriots*. New York: Simon and Schuster, 1988.
Larson, Edward J. *A Magnificent Catastrophe*. New York: Free Press, 2007.
Lee, Mike. Written *Out of History: The Forgotten Founders Who Fought Big Government*. New York: Penguin Books, 2017.
Lewis, James E., Jr., *The Burr Conspiracy: Uncovering the Story of an Early American Crisis*, Princeton: Princeton University Press, 2017.
Lockridge, Ross Franklin. *The Harrisons*. 1941.
Lomask, Milton. *Aaron Burr: The Years from Princeton to Vice President, 1756–1805*. New York: Farrar Straus Giroux, 1979.

Lossing, Benson J. *Pictorial Field Book of the Revolution*. New York: Harper Brothers. 1851.

Maier, Pauline. *American Scripture: Making the Declaration of Independence*. New York: Alfred A. Knopf, Inc., 1997.

McCullough, David. *John Adams*. New York: Simon & Schuster, 2002.

Meltzer, Brad & Josh Mensch. *The First Conspiracy: The Secret Plot to Kill George Washington*. New York: Flat Iron Books. 2018.

Middlekauff, Robert. *The Glorious Cause: The American Revolution, 1763–1789*. Oxford: Oxford University Press, 2005.

Miller, Jr., Arthur P. & Marjorie L. Miller. *Pennsylvania Battlefields and Military Landmarks*. Mechanicsburg, Pennsylvania: Stackpole Books, 2000.

Millett, Allan R. & Peter Maslowski. *For the Common Defense: A Military History of the United States of America*. New York: The Free Press, 1984.

Moore, Charles. *The Family Life of George Washington*. New York: Houghton Mifflin, 1926.

Nagel, Paul C. *The Lees of Virginia: Seven Generations of an American Family*. Oxford: Oxford University Press, 1990.

O'Connell, Robert L. *Revolutionary: George Washington at War*. New York: Random House. 2019.

Racove, Jack N. *Revolutionaries: A New History of the Invention of America*. New York: Houghton Mifflin Harcourt, 2011.

Raphael, Ray. Founding Myths: *Stories That Hide Our Patriotic Past*. New York: MJF Books, 2004.

Rossiter, Clinton. *1787 The Grand Convention*. New York: The Macmillan Company, 1966.

Seymour, Joseph. *The Pennsylvania Associators, 1747–1777*. Yardley, Pennsylvania: Westholme Publishing, LLC. 2012.

Schweikart, Larry & Michael Allen. *A Patriot's History of the United States from Columbus's Great Discovery to the War on Terror*. New York: Penguin, 2004.

Sharp, Arthur G. *Not Your Father's Founders*. Avon, Massachusetts: Adams Media, 2012.

Stahr, Walter. *John Jay: Founding Father*. New York: Diversion Books, 2017.

Taafee, Stephen R. *The Philadelphia Campaign, 1777–1778*. Lawrence, Kansas: University of Kansas Press, 2003.

Tinkcom, Harry Marlin, *The Republicans and the Federalists in Pennsylvania, 1790–1801*. Harrisburg, Pennsylvania: Pennsylvania Historical and Museum Commission. 1950.

Ward, Matthew C. *Breaking the Backcountry: The Seven Years' War in Virginia and Pennsylvania, 1754–1765*. Pittsburgh, Pennsylvania: University of Pittsburgh Press, 2003.

Weisberger, Bernard A. *America Afire: Jefferson, Adams, and the Revolutionary Election of 1800*. New York: HarperCollins, 2000.

Wood, Gordon S. *The Radicalism of the American Revolution*. New York: Vintage Books, 1993.

SOURCES

———. *Empire of Liberty: A History of the Early Republic, 1789–1815*. New York: Penguin Books, 2004.

———. *Revolutionary Characters: What Made the Founders Different*. New York: Penguin Books, 2006.

———. *The Americanization of Benjamin Franklin*. Oxford: Oxford University Press, 2009.

Wright, Benjamin F. *The Federalist: The Famous Papers on the Principles of American Government: Alexander Hamilton, James Madison, John Jay*. New York: Metro Books, 2002.

Zobel, Hiller B. *The Boston Massacre*. New York: W. W. Norton & Company, 1970.

Video Resources:

Guelzo, Allen C. The Great Courses: *America's Founding Fathers* (Course N. 8525). Chantilly, Virginia: The Teaching Company, 2017.

Online Resources:

Archives.gov – for information on the Constitutional Convention.
CauseofLiberty.blogspot.com – for information on Daniel Carroll.
ColonialHall.com – for information about the signers of the Declaration of Independence.
DSDI1776.com – for information on many Founders.
FamousAmericans.net – for information on many Founders.
FindaGrave.com – for burial information, vital statistics and obituaries.
FirstLadies.org – for information on Abigail Adams.
Newspapers.com – Hundreds of newspaper articles were accessed—too numerous to mention here.
NPS.gov – for information on various park sites.
TeachingAmericanHistory.com – for information on Charles Pinckney and George Wythe.
TheHistoryJunkie.com – for information on multiple Founders.
USHistory.org – for information on multiple Founders.
Wikipedia.com – for general historical information.

Index

Adams, John, 1, 11, 24, 34
Alamance, Battle of, 3, 8, 28
Articles of Confederation, v, vi, 16, 18, 20, 35, 37, 44–46
Blount, William, vi, 7–13
Boston, Massachusetts, 4, 19, 26, 28, 49
Burke, Thomas, vi, 14–17
Camden, Battle of, 6, 9, 39–40, 49
Cape Fear, North Carolina, 18, 27
Caswell, Richard, v, 1–6, 16, 39, 49
Charleston, South Carolina, 9, 17, 49
Constitution, US, vi, 6-7, 10, 13, 30, 33, 39, 41, 47, 50
Continental Association, v, 1, 4, 22, 26
Declaration of Independence, v, 20, 22, 26, 29, 32, 35–36
Edenton, North Carolina, 18, 23, 31, 34, 49
Franklin, Benjamin, vi, 9–10, 47, 49
Gates, Horatio, 9, 40,
Greene, Nathanael, 37, 49
Halifax Resolves, 15, 20

Harnett, Cornelius, vi, 15, 18–21
Hewes, Joseph, v, 3–4, 22–25, 36
Hillsborough, North Carolina, 14–15, 17, 26, 28–30, 45
Hooper, William, v, 3–4, 26–30, 36
Iredell, James, vi, 31–34
Jefferson, Thomas, 11–12, 22, 28–29, 41, 50
Laurens, Henry, 37
Madison, James, 41, 46, 50
Nash, Abner, 15, 37
New Bern, North Carolina, 2, 15, 39, 41–42
New York, New York, vi, 47, 50–51
Penn, John, vi, 35–39
Philadelphia, Pennsylvania, v-vi, 4, 9–10, 12–13, 15, 20, 22, 25, 39, 41, 46–50
Spaight, Richard Dobbs, vi, 9, 39–43
Washington, George, 9–10, 12, 31, 33–34, 41
Williams, John, vi, 44–46
Williamson, Hugh, vi, 47–51
Wilmington, North Carolina, 18–21, 25, 27, 29, 38

www.ingramcontent.com/pod-product-compliance
Lightning Source LLC
Chambersburg PA
CBHW011802040426
42449CB00016B/3465